10 Ways to Fund a College Education

Without Giving Up Your Retirement

How to Fund Your Child's – or Grandchild's – Education

H. Roger Daisley
CLU, RHU, CHFC, ACS, FICF, LUTC-F, CFBS, CFS

Blue Horizon Books
www.bluehorizonbooks.com

10 Ways to Fund a College Education
Without Giving Up Your Retirement

All rights reserved. No part of this book may be reproduced or transmitted in any form or by any means, electronic or otherwise, including photocopying, without the express written consent of H. Roger Daisley.

© Copyright 2011   H. Roger Daisley

H. Roger Daisley
HRD Consulting
www.HRD-Consulting.com
631-328-5786
hrdaisley@gmail.com

ISBN: 978-0-578-08864-8

Published by
Blue Horizon Books
www.bluehorizonbooks.com

Cover: *Dawn Daisley Designs*

PRINTED IN THE UNITED STATES OF AMERICA

Table of Contents

INTRODUCTION 7

CHAPTER 1: 10 Ways to Fund a College
Education 11

CHAPTER 2: A Typical American Family 17

CHAPTER 3: Scholarships and Financial Aid 21

CHAPTER 4: 529 Plans 27

CHAPTER 5: Coverdell Education Savings
Account (ESAs) 33

CHAPTER 6: IRAs AND 401(k)s 37

CHAPTER 7: U.S. Savings Bonds /
Education Savings Bonds 41

CHAPTER 8: Uniform Gift to Minors Act /
Uniform Trust to Minors Act (UGMA
/ UTMA) — including "Kiddie Tax"
issues 45

CHAPTER 9: Income and Accumulation
Trusts, or 2503(b) / 2503(c) 49

CHAPTER 10: Hope / American
Opportunity and Lifetime Learning
Credits 51

CHAPTER 11: Tax Techniques to Help
Educational Funding 53

CHAPTER 12: Limited Payment Life
          Insurance Policy 59

CHAPTER 13: Summary 67

Appendix A: The Investment Pyramid 70

Appendix B: Highlights of Education Tax
          Benefits for Tax Year 2010 72

Suggested Reading 74

About H. Roger Daisley 77

An investment in knowledge
pays the best interest.

~ Benjamin Franklin

Please Note

I have made every effort to make this book as complete and accurate as possible on the date of publication. However, tax rules change and proofreaders can miss a typographical error.

This book is not meant to be construed as legal advice, or the last and latest word on financial advice. Therefore, use this book as a general guide and consult a qualified, licensed advisor if you have questions about your specific situation.

All contributors to this book, including myself as author, are in no way liable or responsible to you or any person for any damage or liability caused directly or indirectly by information in this book.

~ H. Roger Daisley

INTRODUCTION

I wrote this book because I have put two children through college, and both my wife and I have pursued graduate degrees as adults. College can be very expensive! I've found that most people put off thinking about it until is almost too late.

It is *never too early* to think about planning for how you are going to fund your child's—or grandchild's—higher education, if you want to help them get the best start possible in their career.

Remember that it is always better to have money and not need it, than to need money and not have it. The time to start planning and saving for college funding is NOW! Then, if it turns out that the money isn't needed or used for college expenses, you will have it available for retirement funds or that retirement home on the lake.

Seek Professional Help!

Over my many years of working in the financial services industry, I became aware of the fact that although there is an abundance of options for families of every income status and situation to receive help in funding a child's college education, most people are not aware of most of these options, including those who are in a position to advise them, such as their tax accountant, investment manager, college financial aid officer or school guidance counselor.

Wouldn't planning and counseling for how to fund a child's education be a welcome addition to financial aid services at high schools and colleges? Wouldn't it be even better to have these services available during grade school as well? Of course! But this kind of counseling is NOT available at most schools and colleges, and when it is, the advisers are rarely well-versed in the kinds of options presented in this book.

I strongly recommend that you review your overall financial plan, including taxes, with an experienced professional who knows educational funding and related tax benefits.

Make sure it's a licensed and experienced specialist because these are not just tax-related issues. Various funding options may impact financial aid qualifications and/or the amounts the child or family is eligible to receive, and a specialist will assure that both funding and tax issues are dealt with appropriately.

Caveats About Investment Funds And Your Plans For Retirement

There are over 72 million Baby Boomers in the U.S. right now, people who were born between the years 1946 and 1964. The oldest of these Boomers turned 65, the "normal" traditional age of retirement, in 2011. The youngest will turn 65 in 2029.

Many have taken early retirement. As of the writing of this book, there are already over 38 million people receiving Social Security income, and many more will be added over the next decade. One of the federal government's solutions to the underfunded Social Security and Medicare systems is to continue raising the age of retirement.

The Social Security system is paying out more money than it is taking in through FICA or Social Security payroll taxes. To put it another way, the estimated cost to provide Social Security and Medicare is in excess of

$70 trillion, an unimaginable number, considering that the entire net worth of the United States is only a little over $54 trillion. Therefore, counting on Social Security as it exists today in terms of retirement age, benefit amounts, cost of living adjustments, and taxation is somewhat precarious.

Many "Think Tank" economists and heads of economic departments at many large colleges and universities are predicting that the stock market growth most Boomers experienced as adults may not be the kind of growth we will experience in the foreseeable future. Remember the not-so-funny jokes during the latest economic crisis about how everyone's 401(k) became a 201(k)?

So, because of the unpredictability of Social Security and of stock market returns, we should consider methods of guaranteeing that money will be there for our children's and grandchildren's education and our eventual retirement.

Another caveat: With many methods for accumulating assets, the assets become the child's when the child reaches 18 or 21. Yet, most parents I've spoken to do not think their children will have the fiscal maturity to manage those assets wisely at that age, when they are still in college or just graduating and—hopefully—starting their careers. Quite frankly, the child can take all the money and host a big fraternity party if that's what they want to do with it. (Not my children, of course!)

Be sure to see the notes in each chapter about other issues specific to each funding option.

And feel free to photocopy the charts in the Appendix which summarize general information about tax benefits and exclusions. These come from IRS publication 970 (with a few modifications by me), and so you might say you've already paid for some of this information in this book with your tax dollars. [1]

---

[1] Always check the current status of income and interest limitations, as tax laws change from year to year. And when considering options like the American Opportunity and Lifetime Learning Credits, note that generally you cannot claim more than one benefit for the same child's educational expense each year.

CHAPTER 1: 10 Ways to Fund a College Education

Figuring out how to finance your child's—or grandchild's—college education is a time-consuming process. You need to do lots of research long before the child is ready to even think about choosing a college, and you need to take into account your retirement plans as well.

It is not only a time-consuming process, but it involves very significant decisions. Higher education may be one of the highest expenses you will have to incur in your entire life. So, obviously, it is a topic that deserves your time and your focus.

And yet—many people spend more time planning a two-week vacation than they spend in their entire lifetime planning their own financial future, including significant financial events such as the cost of a good education.

Planning for a child's education is not an isolated incidence of financial planning, just as investment plans are not complete financial plans, nor is tax planning or mortgage or other loan planning a complete financial plan, in and of itself.

My point is: When you are planning how to fund your child's—or grandchild's education—you will want to take all sorts of other, seemingly related, factors into account and make sure your plans are coordinated. It is important to have an overall plan, and to take enough time to do it right.

The costs to pay for a child's college education can vary significantly—from almost half a million dollars to attend an Ivy League or elite private school, to tens of thousands for state universities.

Ironically, you may very well find that the expensive private school will cost you less out of pocket than the much cheaper state school. This is because private schools tend to give out more financial aid dollars—and that is because they are almost always much better funded than state schools.

Another consideration is the fact that at private schools, the percentage of students that graduate in four years is significantly higher than students at state schools.

There are many ways to save and pay for your children's—or grandchildren's—education. And many have some favorable tax ramifications.

My focus here is on 10 key methods, some of which are well-known and a few that are frequently overlooked:

1. Scholarships and Financial Aid[2]
2. 529 Plans
3. College Education Savings Accounts (ESAs)
4. IRAs and 401(k)s
5. U.S. Savings Bonds
6. Uniform Gift to Minors/Uniform Trust to Minors (UGMA/UTMA)
7. Income and Accumulation Trusts: 2503(b) and 2503(c)

---

[2] Options numbered 1, 8, and 9 are specifically for older children who are in the process of applying to college, have already been accepted, or have started attending college.

8. Hope/American Opportunity and Lifetime Learning Tax Credits[2]
9. Tax Techniques to Help Educational Funding[2]
10. Life Insurance Options

Some of these may be familiar. But it's very likely that you haven't thought of all of these methods before now.

For instance, various tax advantaged vehicles, including life insurance, seem to be overlooked as college funding options. So consider all possible options and how they may apply to you and your family. But be sure to review your options with a knowledgeable financial professional *prior* to choosing one, or even several, accumulation plans because regulations and tax laws change.

Why Use A Professional?

Tax laws change on a regular basis, and many of these affect educational funding options. A professional has to stay on top of these regulatory changes, as part of their professional licensing.

To the non-professional, it can be quite confusing. Do you even qualify for a particular option? What are the financial and tax ramifications of choosing one option over another? How does the choice of one funding option effect other sources of financial aid?

They say a picture is worth a thousand words. A colleague of mine shared this diagram from the U.S. Office of Education. He gave it a rather ironic title: Financial Aid Is Easy!

The diagram attempts to "simplify" the processes of the student financial aid delivery system using a flow chart. Instead, it illustrates clearly how complicated it actually is.

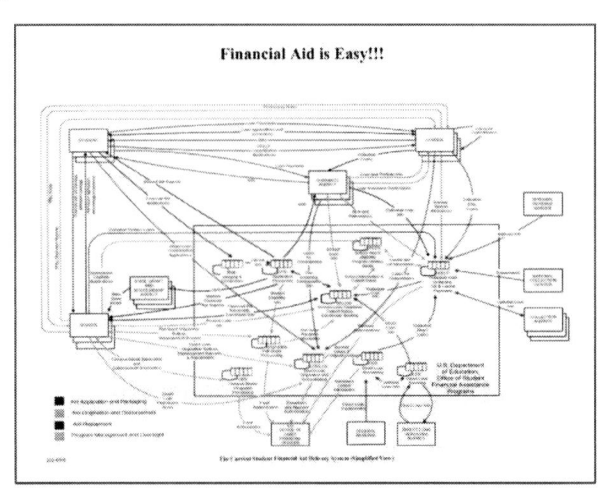

Courtesy of Andy Lockwood, J.D. (www.andylockwood.com)

Yes, it's complicated. And if you have the time to devote yourself full-time to studying every aspect of college education funding—starting when the child is still a toddler—you just might gather the know-how to figure it all out.

But if you don't have the leisure or the inclination to devote a lot of time to becoming a professional who is not only well-versed in this subject, but licensed—well, that's why you go to a professional who has already devoted many years of their career to learning about education funding, someone who has earned the credentials and experience to advise others.

H. Roger Daisley

CHAPTER 2: A Typical American Family

My clients "Mike and Judy"[3] are a fairly typical two-earner suburban couple in their mid-40's living in a bedroom community near New York City.

Now, we all know that in reality, there is no such thing as a "typical" American family. Today, many parents are in their second marriages and there are "blended" families and many single-parent families. There are fewer situations in which multiple generations are living under one roof together. Families that used to have four, five, six or more children are now having only 2.03 children.

But I think it helps to imagine how these 10 options for funding a college education might be apply to a "typical" family. So for that purpose, I will be referring to "Mike and Judy" and their family throughout this book.

"Mike and Judy" And Their Family[3]

Judy is a research editor earning about $95,000. Mike owns a growing online business that allows him to work from home. He clears about $55,000 annually. This may sounds wealthy to some, I'm sure, but in the New York metro area we are talking middle-class.

Mike and Judy's children are Michelle, 17, and Sarah, 12. And they now have a one-year-old, Jane. This is a

---

[3] "Mike and Judy" and their family are pseudonyms, used to represent a composite of families I have advised over the years.

second marriage for both the husband and wife. Michelle, the oldest daughter, is a top 10 percentile student who took early admission to a northeast public university. She wants to major in English. She received some merit aid, but the net cost of attending that university is $33,000 annually after a "tuition discount." There isn't much free cash available, considering the family will be funding college for more than one child.

Additional Complicating Factors

Sarah, Mike and Judy's middle child, who is still in junior high school, has a diagnosed learning disability and is receiving specialized counseling under the supervision of a therapist. The annual cost for this is $12,000. Except for a few visits each year, the coverage available from Judy's medical insurance at work is essentially zero. So at present, this is an after-tax family expense.

In addition, Mike and Judy are subject to the alternative minimum tax, the tax code scourge of middle-class taxpayers. As a result, they have to add back into the tax calculation their mortgage interest—one of the "preference items" which limits the effect of their tax deductions. Mike hates to borrow anyway and he is very concerned about saddling his kids with debt upon graduation.

Throw in the piano lessons at $3,000 annually, add graduate degree courses for Judy, a set of braces here and there, and babysitters for the baby, and you've got the typical house-rich, soon to be cash-poor American family.

And on top of everything else, they find a college financing system and federal methodology that considers them not to have financial need, at least while only one child is in college.

The Grandparents

The New York Times ran an article a while back, quoting a USC professor who had informally surveyed his students about how their education was being paid. To his great surprise, grandparents were firmly ensconced in third position as a source of funds, behind parental support and scholarships—and ahead of borrowing.

The author concluded that many grandparents are a bit better off than they thought they would be in retirement.

That is certainly the case for Mike's parents, George and Lydia. With pension, social security and investment income, George and Lydia are in good enough financial shape to visit regularly and to dote on the three grand-daughters, Michelle, Sarah, and Jane.

Included in their assets are some old stocks that George had inherited from his dad, Mike's grandfather. The stocks contribute very little income, but their value appreciated considerably, since they were held for 50-plus years in a solid blue chip company that has stood the test of time.

Most importantly, the grandparents wanted to help finance their grand-daughters' education, and asked me for ideas about how to go about it.

H. Roger Daisley

CHAPTER 3: Scholarships and Financial Aid

This seems to be the obvious place to start, and there are several ways to look at the prospects for scholarships and financial aid, depending upon your "plan" for your children.

Plan A

Make sure your child excels at academics, athletics, music, art, science—preferably all of these areas—while also participating in a significant charitable activity, an internship at a prestigious institution in an industry the student hopes to enter, and otherwise proving to be a solid citizen, someone an institution of higher learning wants to recruit to their ranks.

In other words, plan to become a "Tiger Mom" or Tiger Dad, making a full-time career out of helping your child succeed.

There's one big problem with this plan: There are very, very few "full boats." It is much more common for scholarships and financial aid packages to be awarded in sums of $100, rather than $55,000.

According to various sources, only 1% to 3% of all college costs for all students attending college are paid for by scholarships.[4]

You can't assume that even if your child is an outstanding scholar, athlete, or artist, they will get a full ride at any college or university, especially the one of their choice.

---

[4] See especially Lockwood, *How to Pay "Wholesale" For College*.

Plan B

If you don't expect your child to be winning the Olympics or a Nobel or Pulitzer prize any time soon, or inventing the next Facebook or Google, you will need to demonstrate a *need* for scholarship funds.

It's not just a matter of pleading poverty—if you are solidly middle class, and your child has been accepted to Harvard or Stanford, you are going to need to find supplemental funds to pay for it.

However, do **NOT** assume that even if your family income is over $300,000 you won't qualify for financial aid.

Be prepared to apply for scholarships and financial aid of any and all kinds, even if you have to hire a consultant in this field to help you find your way through the thicket of information and forms.

For instance, there is the "FAFSA," a form normally used for public schools and the "CSS," a form for private schools. Some schools want both and there are significant differences. The Title IV Financial Aid Act (1965) itself is 1,100 pages of small print

Keep in mind that the high school guidance counselor, the college financial aid officer and your accountant are **NOT** necessarily the people to provide that help. This is a highly specialized field. Your CPA may offer to help complete the tax forms for you using standard software, but some of the education funding options addressed in this book actually count against you when applying for financial aid. And it's not part of your CPA's job and/or experience to know how to finesse these finer points.

Plan NOW!

Be prepared to pay for all or most of your child's college education, even if the child receives a decent scholarship. That scholarship may not last because the child may not meet the key criteria to maintain the scholarship through four (or more) years of undergraduate school. The school may come up with a reason to withdraw support, unrelated to the student's performance, once the child has started school within their system.

As an example, my youngest daughter was at a major university working on her bachelor's degree. My oldest daughter was working on her masters, and my wife was working on her doctorate. Despite all these scholars in the family, we qualified for only $250 of the favorable tuition low-interest Stafford loans.

For those of you who are not familiar with Stafford loans, they are characterized by the following traits:

- Low fixed-interest rates, as low as 4.5%
- Increased borrowing limits—up to $20,500 per year, depending on the degree status and years in school
- No payments while enrolled in school
- Acceptance is not based on credit

My youngest daughter was offered an $8,000 annual academic scholarship at a prestigious university. However, this scholarship was retroactively withdrawn one month prior to the end of her first semester.

We had filed our taxes late that year because I had moved from one company in one state to another company in another state, and it took a while for all the paperwork to catch up with us. When we filed our taxes in the fall of that year, we sent a copy to our daughter's university.

That's when the Powers That Be at the university decided that her "academic" scholarship was now a "needs-based" scholarship, and that she no longer needed that money. And nothing could have been farther from the truth, with three in the family in college, the costs of moving still catching up with us, and my income had gone down, not up.

We quickly found we weren't the only victims of this "bait and switch" tactic—there was a flood of news coverage about major colleges and universities doing the same thing to many other families across the nation—using "academic" scholarships to attract the best students, and then withdrawing the scholarship for vague or fine-print reasons.[5]

Whether or not your child (or grandchild) qualifies for a scholarship, it's best to have your own plan for funding their college education. For one thing, you won't know about scholarship offers until their senior year in high school. And if no offers are forthcoming, it may be too late to go back and come up with alternative funding plans.

---

[5] See especially: "Tips to Avoid Bait & Switch in the World of Financial Aid," by Doug A. Schantz, www.cheapscholar.org, March 11, 2010.

Basic Formula And Terminology Used In Determining Financial Aid

It starts with this formula: COA – EFC = Need

COA is Cost of Attendance, and EFC is Expected Family Contribution. In order to apply for financial aid, you'll need to become familiar with several additional terms. FAFSA is the Free Application for Federal Student Aid, the federal form most state schools require you to complete to establish your financial need.

CSS is the College Scholarship Service, the form that most private schools need you to complete to establish need for private schools.

And of course some schools require both.

You are not required to get help in order to complete these forms, but it might be a good idea. For example, if you own a business and the form asks you to list the value of your business, you might assume that you have to put down a number which may be in the hundreds of thousands. However, in the 1,100 page instructions of the Title IV Financial Aid Act, it states that if you have fewer than 100 employees, you can list the value of your business at "0." Yes—zero.

I am sure you can appreciate that this factor alone could cost you many financial aid dollars.

Mike & Judy and Family

I advised Mike and Judy to talk to their counselors at Michelle's high school, and to look into every organization they belonged to—church, social, community and fraternal organizations—and to have Michelle herself do research to identify possible scholarship opportunities. I urged them to apply for anything and everything Michelle was eligible for.

I also told them not to assume they would not qualify for aid, despite earning a solid middle-class family income. And I suggested that they look into hiring a specialist to help them complete the necessary forms.

SUMMARY

Positives: If your child has outstanding talents in areas such athletics, academics, music, art and/or leadership, there is a chance that they will be eligible for a scholarship. In addition, there is a multitude of small, sometimes obscure scholarships available if you do your homework. And most families can qualify for at least some financial aid.

Negatives: Very few students receive full scholarships to cover all college expenses—all tuition, room, board and books, much less the costs for food and clothing—for a full four years. Scholarships received may be withdrawn, at the discretion of the college. Applying for financial aid can be a confusing process with obscure rules.

CHAPTER 4: 529 Plans

A 529 Plan allows the parents to contribute into a fund for the purpose of saving money for college. The beauty of these plans—and there are hundreds of different plans—is that there is no federal tax deduction for the contributions into the 529 Plan, although some states provide a state income tax deduction if the 529 Plan is incorporated in your state of residence.[6]

So, in other words, the money contributed to a 529 Plan accumulates in the plan free of income tax. You could be making money, but without paying tax on the profits.

In addition, the annual Gift Tax Exclusion is $13,000 per person contributing to the plan. In other words, a parent or grandparent, or anyone for that matter, may make a gift to the child of $13,000 annually and that gift is not counted as income for the recipient (the child).

Also, when you take the money out of a 529 Plan for allowable college expenses, you will probably incur no income tax.

Additionally, if you have the resources, you can contribute the first five years' contributions when you initiate the plan, thus earning more interest immediately, and yet this additional profit on your investment will most likely not be taxed.

The 529 Plan is one of the newest investment vehicles to come along in years, and most investment

---

[6] For complete information on deductions allowed in your own state, refer to the Suggested Reading section in the Appendix for sources of information.

companies, banks and insurance companies sell their clients a mutual fund-based 529 Plan.

Investments can include growth funds invested in the stock market, bond funds, and fixed income funds, sometimes with guaranteed principle. It is an investment that can produce profits (if the stock market isn't headed downhill) and is worth considering, under the right circumstances. Some states also allow a state income tax deduction for their state plans and any independent plan incorporated in that state.

In addition, many states allow you to transfer funds remaining in a plan set up for one child, to another family member (a sibling, yourself or your spouse, even first cousins), if your child doesn't use all the money in the course of attaining their college degree.

Caveats

- Some plans and some states limit how much you may contribute annually into your 529 Plan. If more than $13,000 is contributed (the amount allowed under the Gift Tax Exclusion) it has to be deemed a "reasonable amount" by the IRS—for instance, the cost of tuition at an Ivy League school, which will certainly be more than $13,000.
- If you withdraw the funds for purposes other than allowable college expenses, you will have to claim the profit as ordinary income and pay a 10% penalty tax.
- It is also important to note that these funds are usually invested in mutual funds. In an economy like we have now, that may mean you may

actually lose the money you invest. So, the market risk cannot be overlooked.

- It is also important to note that 529 Plan assets count against you when filing for needs-based financial aid. The 529 Plan is considered an asset of the parent by state schools and is usually considered an asset of the child by most private schools, as indicated on the forms.

- You are allowed to contribute the first five years contribution into the plan when you initiate your 529 Plan. However, if you die during this first five-year period, your estate will have to pay gift taxes on any amount over the annual exclusion amount, which is currently $13,000.

- If the primary income earner dies or becomes permanently disabled, the family would experience a significant income loss and may have to discontinue putting money into the Plan.

- In the case of death or disability, the family may have to withdraw funds from the Plan, which would result in a 10% tax penalty.

Not only do you have investment risk, but this option reduces the amount of financial aid your child will qualify for. And this is true of many educational funding plans that are based on an investment plan.

Types Of 529 Plans

There are several hundred versions of 529 Plans, but they boil down to two basic types:

- Independent
- State-sponsored pre-paid plan

The independent plans are sold by almost every mutual fund company and your child is not limited to any specific school in any state. Here, given the current economic climate, you would want to make sure you choose a company that had historically higher returns for the last 10 years, which is difficult in this economy.

The state-sponsored plans, usually called "Contract" or "Unit" plans, allow you to put money into the plan and prepay the college expenses for state schools and some out-of-state schools. (The rules vary by state, and they do change from time to time.) These plans may not cover the cost of out-of-state or private schools, and you are limited to putting money into the specific plan sponsored by your state.

Mike & Judy and Family

Simply put, there are well over 280 of these 529 Plans in this country, and saving for college is a good thing, whether it's the parents, aunts, uncles or grandparents investing their money for their college-bound child, niece, nephew, grandson or daughter.

529 Plans seem to get lots of attention because most every investment company, bank, or insurance company can sell this plan. President George W. Bush put forth this plan to help encourage parents to save for college and to stimulate the economy.

However, I advised Mike and Judy to carefully weigh the pros and cons of the 529 Plan, especially if they were concerned about economic conditions and the possible rate of return on investments. George and Lydia were concerned about the possible estate tax for their son Mike, if they died before a 529 Plan could be used for what it was intended to be used for—their granddaughters' educations.

In addition, Mike and Judy weren't happy with the fact that the assets in the 529 Plan would count against them when they applied for financial aid for Michelle's college tuition.

SUMMARY

Positives: The income in a 529 Plan accumulates income tax-free, and in some states, there is a state income tax deduction. You can start the fund with the first five years' contributions made at the inception of the plan, and contribute up to $13,000 per year, per child, per contributor, with no penalties from the IRS. If funds remain when the child graduates, they can be transferred to another sibling, a parent and even first cousins.

Negatives: Return on investment depends on how well the stock market is doing. If the fund owner dies, there may be an estate tax. If the owner contributed those first five years of deposits into the Plan, and then dies prior to the end of those first five years, there may also be gift taxes. These plans can only be used for educational expenses, and count against you, as an asset, when applying for financial aid.

H. Roger Daisley

CHAPTER 5: Coverdell Education Savings Account (ESAs)

The Coverdell Education Savings Account, commonly known as the "ESA" allows a $2,000 contribution per year per child—not enough to cover tuition even at the most inexpensive state college or even most culinary institutes. However, the ESA is not restricted to just college expenses.

Established in 2002, the ESA quickly became a very attractive educational savings vehicle for many parents because a number of K-12 expenses were added to the list of qualified expenses.

In addition, withdrawals for college costs are not reported as student or parent income, as long as they are used for qualified educational expenses. So, essentially, ESA account income is accumulated income tax-free.

In fact, even if you like the 529 Plan or other educational funding plans you may decide also to make an annual $2,000 contribution for each child into an ESA/Coverdell account to be used for pre-college educational expenses, like secondary school.

Caveats[7]

- Only $2,000 in total contributions per year is allowed, otherwise a penalty will be imposed.
- Be very careful when accounts are established by different family members for the same child, that

---

[7] This information can be found in IRS Publication 970.

the total contributions do not exceed the limit for the year.

- Tax law prohibits ESA funding once the beneficiary reaches age 18, and the account must be fully withdrawn by the time the beneficiary reaches age 30, or else it will be subject to tax and penalties.

- The balance in the account, if any, after payouts for educational expenses, will eventually be distributed to your child—and only your child. You cannot simply refund the account back to yourself, or another relative, as you can with most 529 Plans.

- The relatively low contribution limit means that even a small annual maintenance fee charged by the financial institution holding your ESA could significantly affect your overall investment return.

- The ESA is on equal footing, negatively speaking, with the 529 Plan when applying for federal financial aid—the account is considered an asset of the account custodian, whether it is the parent, grandparent or child.

- Coordinating withdrawals from an ESA with other tax benefits can be tricky, in particular the Hope/American Opportunity or Lifetime Learning credits (see Chapter 10).

- Unless Congress acts, (as of this writing, Congress has NOT acted) certain ESA benefits will expire in 2012. Additionally, K-12 expenses will no longer qualify, the annual contribution limit will be reduced to $500, and withdrawals will not be tax-free in any year in which a Hope/American Opportunity credit or Lifetime Learning credit is claimed for the beneficiary.

Mike & Judy and Family

Though the ESA might provide a small benefit for Sarah, it wouldn't provide any relief for the burden of Michelle's educational expenses, since there is little time for the funds to accumulate.

However, I told Mike and Judy that the ESA might be a good tool for Jane's educational expenses, since she is so young. There would be plenty of time for the accumulation of funds, both for a private secondary school, if they decide to go that route, as well as for one of the better colleges.

SUMMARY

Positives: ESA funds can be used for a wide variety of educational expenses, not just for college, but also for K-12 expenses. Withdrawals for legitimate educational expenses are not taxed as income.

Negatives: Contributions are limited to $2,000 per year, per child—and accounts must be kept carefully. Funds must be distributed to the beneficiary between the ages of 18 and 30. Maintenance fees may negate interest earnings if the market isn't doing well. This entire option may expire soon, or be drastically reduced, unless Congress acts to extend the current benefits.

H. Roger Daisley

CHAPTER 6: IRAs AND 401(k)s

Generally, when it comes to IRAs and 401(k) accounts, you can borrow up to $50,000 or half your account balance, whichever is less, for educational expense purposes, and you have up to five years to repay the loan, plus interest, usually through payroll deductions.

Interest rates vary from plan to plan, but a typical charge is the prime rate plus one percentage point.

If your age is at least 59½ or older, you escape the 10% tax penalty for taking a withdrawal.

Caveats

- Not all plans allow for loans for educational expenses.
- If you take money out of your IRA or 401(k) without repaying it, it will be taxed as ordinary income. In addition, you will have to pay a penalty of 10% of the lump sum withdrawn—unless you are 59½ years old or older.
- If you take the money from your IRA or 401(k) as a loan, the loan proceeds aren't taxable, but you do have to repay the loan with interest, which is not tax deductible, and that must be done within 5 years.
- If you switch jobs, the loan must be paid back right away, typically within 60 days of the time you leave. If you don't have the cash to pay off the loan, the loan balance will be considered a taxable distribution, which means you would owe tax, plus the 10% penalty if you're under age 59½.

"Hardship" Withdrawals From A 401(k)

As a last resort, there's always the "Hardship Withdrawal" from a 401(k). This is another way to get money out of your workplace 401(k), but it's not easy. Again, the plan doesn't have to offer this option, even though about 95% do offer it.

Getting a Hardship Withdrawal isn't just a simple matter of saying you're financially pressed and could use the money. IRS rules stipulate that you must demonstrate "an immediate and heavy" financial need. What constitutes a hardship is not clear, but it would take some extreme circumstances—perhaps not as extreme as having had all your possessions lost in Hurricane Katrina, but along those lines.

Paying college tuition and related educational expenses does qualify as an "immediate and heavy" financial need. However, the rules also state that the distribution must be necessary to satisfy that financial need and that you have *no other way of meeting it.*

In other words, you cannot get a Hardship Withdrawal if there are other resources you can access to pay your kids' college bills, and the IRS expects you to exhaust these options before resorting to the Hardship Withdrawal:

- Dissolve or borrow on other investments and assets, such as insurance policies
- Apply for a home equity loan
- Take a loan from your 401(k) plan, if that is allowed.

The size of a Hardship Withdrawal is generally limited to the amount you've contributed to the plan, although in some cases you may also be able to withdraw from the funds contributed by your employer, if your employer contributed any funds.

The withdrawal is taxable and subject to the 10% early-withdrawal penalty as well, which can really whittle down how much you'll have left to apply to college expenses.

There are some instances where the penalty is waived, but education expenses don't qualify. For details on rules and regulations surrounding Hardship Withdrawals, you'll probably have to apply in writing for a Hardship Withdrawal and your employer will decide whether you qualify. And remember, the plan administrators are accountable to both the Department of Labor and the IRS, so they cannot be very liberal in allowing Hardship Withdrawals.

All in all, a Hardship Withdrawal should be considered only as a last resort, not only because you may not qualify, but because it can seriously derail your retirement prospects:

- With a loan, at least you're putting the money you borrowed, plus interest, back into your account.
- You are not allowed to restore Hardship Withdrawal funds, period. So that money, plus whatever it would have earned, is lost as far as your retirement is concerned.

Clearly, a 401(k) loan is a much better option than a Hardship Withdrawal. But you should investigate other options before digging into your 401(k), even for a loan.

Mike & Judy and Family

The IRA / 401(k) loan option would almost always be a last choice for any family, including Mike and Judy's.

And the idea of taking a Hardship Withdrawal would be an even worse choice. The parents will need to retire one day, and this money is for that purpose. If it is all spent for college expenses, how will they be able to afford to retire? Also, the miracle of compound interest will have ceased to work for them; they will no longer be earning interest on those savings for their retirement.

As I advise all families, college funding and retirement planning should be done in connection with one another, as these are some of the biggest expenses the family will encounter in their lifetime.

Ultimately, Mike and Judy were lucky enough not to have to borrow from their retirement accounts—though they did weigh it seriously as an option.

SUMMARY

Positives: For grandparents, who are more likely to meet the age criteria, there is no penalty for taking a loan from their IRA or 401(k) plan. Up to $50,000 (or half the account balance) may be borrowed for educational expenses, and they will have five years to repay the amount borrowed to restore retirement funds.

Negatives: Withdrawals that are taken from these plans and not paid back will be counted as ordinary income and taxed as such. If you are under age 59 ½ you will have to pay an additional penalty of 10%. When you re-pay loan proceeds, you are charged an interest rate (for instance 5%) that negates what the funds would have earned through compounded interest (for instance 2%) if they had not been withdrawn, creating a net loss of (for instance) 7% total.

CHAPTER 7: U.S. Savings Bonds / Education Savings Bonds

The U.S. Savings Bond / Education Tax Exclusion permits qualified taxpayers to exclude from their gross income all or part of the interest paid upon the redemption of eligible Series EE and I Bonds issued after 1989, when the bond owner pays qualified higher education expenses at an eligible institution.

In other words, you can use a U.S. Savings Bonds toward your child's education and exclude all the interest income earned from your federal income. This is sometimes known as the Tax-Free Interest for Education Program.

When purchasing bonds to be used for education, you do NOT have to declare at the time of purchase that you will be using them for education purposes.

You can also choose not to use the bonds for education if you so choose at a later date.

Caveats

- Qualified higher education expenses incurred by you, your spouse, or your child (basically: tuition and fees related to course work) have to be incurred in the same calendar year the bonds are cashed in.

- Parents must be at least 24 years old when they purchase the bonds.

- The amount may not be enough to pay for college tuition and other college expenses.

- Only Series EE or I Bonds issued in 1990 and later apply. "Older" bonds cannot be exchanged towards newer bonds.

- The bonds must be registered in your name, and not the child's name. A child cannot be listed as a co-owner on the bond.

- The child can be a beneficiary on the bond and the education exclusion can still apply.

- If you are married, a joint return MUST be filed to qualify for the education exclusion.

- You are required to report both the principal and the interest from the bonds to pay for qualified expenses. Use Form 8815 to exclude interest for college tuition.

- In tax year 2010, for single taxpayers, the tax exclusion begins to be reduced with a $70,100 modified adjusted gross income and is eliminated for adjusted gross incomes of $85,100 and above. For married taxpayers filing jointly, the tax exclusion begins to be reduced with a $105,100 modified adjusted gross income and is eliminated for adjusted gross incomes of $135,100 and above.

- These income limitations apply to the year you use the bonds, and NOT when you purchase the bonds. Currently, the interest rate is only 0.6%.

Mike & Judy and Family

As it turned out, Mike and Judy's joint earnings were too high to qualify under the current regulations, but the grandparents' joint income was low enough—and they had lower income needs as well. So, they considered this option seriously.

However, with the low 0.6% interest rate, they decided that other college funding concepts were more appropriate.

SUMMARY

Positives: Income earned on bonds is tax-free, if used for educational purposes.

Negatives: The interest rates are relatively low, and the tax rules are very specific as to ownership, use, and income limits.

H. Roger Daisley

CHAPTER 8: Uniform Gift to Minors Act / Uniform Trust to Minors Act (UGMA / UTMA) — including "Kiddie Tax" issues

The Uniform Gift to Minors Act (UMGA) established a simple way for a minor to own securities without requiring the services of an attorney to prepare trust documents or the court appointment of a trustee. (A "trust" is legal relationship in which one party, known as the trustor, gives to a person or organization, known as the trustee, the right to hold and invest assets or property on behalf of a third party, known as the beneficiary.) The terms of the UGMA are established by a state statute instead of a trust document.

The Uniform Transfer to Minors Act (UTMA) is similar, but also allows minors to own other types of property, such as real estate, fine art, patents and royalties, and for the transfers to occur through inheritance. UTMA is slightly more flexible than UGMA.

Custodial accounts are most often established at banks and brokerage firms and insurance companies. To establish a custodial account, the donor must appoint a custodian (trustee) and provide the name and social security number of the minor. The donor irrevocably gifts the money to the trust. The money then belongs to the minor but is controlled by the custodian until the minor reaches the age of trust termination. (The age of trust termination is 18 to 21, depending on the state and whether it is an UGMA or an UTMA. Most UGMAs end at 18 and most UTMAs at 21, but it does depend on the state.)

The custodian has the fiduciary responsibility to manage the money in a prudent fashion for the benefit of the minor.

Any money in custodial accounts for which you are the custodian will be counted as part of your taxable estate if you are the legal guardian of the child and the child has not yet reached the age of trust termination.

It is important to title the account correctly. An "In Trust For" account, also known as a "Totten Trust" or guardian account, is not a UGMA/UTMA account. It is a revocable transfer that passes to the beneficiary without probate upon the death of the donor.

Caveats

- The costs involved in setting up a trust are not inconsequential.
- The first $950 of trust income is tax-free, and the second $950 is taxed at the child's income tax rate, which is almost always lower than the parents' tax rate.
- The benefits are minimal—after $1,900 of income, the rest of the income is taxed at the parents' tax rate.
- Additionally, the money becomes the child's at their age of majority, usually 18 or 21, depending upon the child's respective state. (Most states consider 18 the majority age.).
- As with other plans mentioned previously where investments are used (529's, ESAs, Savings Bonds, 401(k)s), the money is considered an asset of the child or parent, either directly or indirectly when

applying for financial aid, which almost always reduces the amount of financial aid for which the family might be eligible.

Stay Tuned

The Kiddie Tax may come under increasing scrutiny—the current Administration sent signals recently (Spring of 2011) that it wants to raise the income tax on all amounts earned by children, and not just those amounts over $1900.

Mike & Judy and Family

The cost of establishing a trust is so significant that, in Mike and Judy's case, it would negate any tax savings. It was clearly not a good choice for their situation—or, for that matter, the grandparents' situation.

SUMMARY

Positives: The first $950 of trust income is tax-free; the second $950 is taxed at the child's income tax rate, which will usually be less than the parents' rate.

Negatives: The tax benefits are minimal. Funds remaining in the plan become the child's at majority, whether they decide to attend college or not. It is very possible that the income tax benefit will be phased out in the present Administration.

CHAPTER 9: Income and Accumulation Trusts, or 2503(b) / 2503(c)

Internal Revenue Code 2503(b) and 2503(c) expressly permit gifts in trust for the benefit of a minor, which also qualify for the annual gift tax exclusion. (See also page 58)

In fact, each trust is expected to make annual (or more frequent) distributions to the child. And each has specific rules about the distribution of the trust when the child reaches age 21:

- With a 2503(c) trust, the assets must be distributed when the child is age 21.

- With the 2503(b) trust, the assets of the trust *do not* have to be distributed when the child reaches age 21.

The 2503(c) trust is best suited for situations where the donor (usually the parents or grandparents) want a more flexible form of ownership than is available with the UGMA, such as paying for college tuition.

In addition, the trustee can make distributions *on behalf of* the minor—for instance, directly to an educational institution—rather than having to make the distribution to the minor directly.

Caveats

- If the trust income is allowed to accumulate because annual distributions weren't made, taxes must be paid on the accumulated income at the trust tax rates.

Mike & Judy and Family

This option can be attractive to grandparents with money, or parents who are well off, or who have highly appreciated assets, or who own a business and want to protect the assets of that business for the child's or grandchild's education. And Mike does have his own business, so I advised him to consider this option.

If his business was sued, the assets in the trust would be protected, and therefore the funds that were earmarked for the children's college education would be protected.

Although he hasn't acted on this option yet, since his business has continued to grow steadily, Mike hasn't ruled the Trust option out.

SUMMARY

Positives: With these trusts, the custodian (parent or grandparent) has more control over how the money is distributed to the child. Funds don't have to be distributed with the (b) trust at any particular age, and with the (c) trust, they do not have to be distributed until the child reaches 21, rather than 18 like many other plans.

Negatives: Some funds from the 2503(c) trust must be distributed annually, or the trust custodian must pay taxes on the accumulated funds at trust tax rates.

CHAPTER 10: Hope / American Opportunity and Lifetime Learning Credits

The Hope/American Opportunity, and Lifetime Learning credits are dollar-for-dollar tax credits, currently up to $2,000 per year. The education doesn't have to be part of a degree program or certificate-granting program, though the tax credit can be used for undergraduate, postgraduate, or professional studies.

These options are tax credits. A tax credit reduces your tax payment, whereas a tax deduction reduces your taxable income. Tax credits are better than tax deductions.

Note that the Hope has been replaced by the American Opportunity. If you have already taken Hope tax credits, these will count the same as the American Opportunity credits, despite the fact that Hope has been phased out, thereby reducing the number of years (a total of four) you can claim the American Opportunity Credit.

If you have more than one child, you can claim the tax credit for each, and if it makes sense, you can claim a one program for one child, and a different program for the other.

If you are in a lower income bracket, these are specifically designed for you.

Caveats

- You cannot claim both the American Opportunity and the Lifetime Learning credits in the same year for the same child.

- For each child, you may only claim tax credits for a total of four years.

- These tax benefits are limited to families earning below certain limits, and the numbers (income levels, amount of tax credit allowed) tend to change from year to year.[8]

Mike & Judy and Family

For Mike and Judy, this wasn't even an option they could consider, as their annual earnings were too high for them to qualify.

SUMMARY

Positives: Ideal for lower-income families. Receive dollar-for-dollar tax credits, rather than a tax deduction, for each child.

Negatives: Only available for lower-income families. Can only be used for four tax years for each child.

---

[8] More information can be found by going to www.irs.gov and accessing Publication 970.

CHAPTER 11: Tax Techniques to Help Educational Funding

As you may have begun to realize, there are all sorts of ways to help fund your child's—or grandchild's—higher education, if you do the right planning. So far, I have been talking mainly about investment vehicles, such as mutual funds and bonds.

A family should also know that, with a little planning, Uncle Sam is willing to help them more than they would have thought. And sometimes some of the best options are right under your nose, or in this case, sitting right across the dining room table.

Let's go back to our typical family, Mike and Judy. As mentioned, Mike and Judy are a two-earner suburban couple in their mid-40's living in a bedroom community near New York City. Judy is a research editor earning about $95,000. Mike owns a growing online business that allows him to work from home and he clears about $55,000 annually. In metro New York this means their family is middle-class.

Mike and Judy's children are 17, 12, and 1. The oldest daughter, Michelle, was soon to be heading off to a northeast public university to major in English. Sarah, Mike and Judy's middle daughter, who is still in junior high school, has a diagnosed learning disability, and is receiving therapy. The baby of the family, Jane, is still several years away from entering nursery school.

There are the usual other factors straining their budget—the alternative minimum tax, piano lessons, braces, babysitters—but on the positive side, Mike's parents George and Lydia are a bit better off than they thought they would be in retirement. Most importantly, the grandparents wanted to help finance their granddaughters' education, and asked me for ideas about how to go about it.

A "Tax Scholarship"

There isn't really such a thing as a "tax scholarship," but that's how I like to think of it. These are actually deductions allowed by the IRS that can help families pay for a child's college education.

In their present situation, the combined annual incomes of Judy and Mike make them ineligible for nearly all of those major tax benefits that I have mentioned so far.

So what I call a "tax scholarship" is an essential consideration. By "shifting and gifting," many small business owners change some college expenses from after-tax expenses, to pre-tax expenses, using the following business practices:

- Hire a college-bound child in the business to do internet research, database management and other computer duties (many of which she can perform while away at school). The annual salary would be tax deductible. You could employ your child for office and tech support, or marketing, presentation design and preparation, web design and management—all depending upon their own area of expertise and interest.

- Hire younger children for general home office work—filing, emptying waste baskets, running errands. That would also be deductible.

- Create an educational reimbursement plan for your employees that allows workers age 21 and over to receive education expense reimbursements as tax-free income. (Mike creates a medical reimbursement plan at his business that pays all medical expenses of his employees—in this case, family members—that are not reimbursed from other sources. These are legitimate expenses to the business without being considered income to the employee.)

Tax-Free Gift From The Grandparents

In addition, the grandparents may give each of their grandchildren $13,000, the current annual tax-free gift limit. That's $26,000 per grandchild if each grandparent contributes $13,000 to each child. And if that $13,000 is in stock or mutual funds, the grandchildren may then sell the stock or funds and use the proceeds for college, along with their wages earned from working in the family business.

As you may remember, in the case of the grandparents, George and Lydia, they had some old stocks that George had inherited from his dad, Mike's grandfather. And though the stocks don't contribute much income, their value appreciated quite a bit over the years.

The basis for determining the value of non-cash gifts is the original amount paid for the stock or other property, and not the current value as it grew over time. If the grandparent cashed in on the stock or mutual funds themselves, they would have to pay a capital gain tax on the profit, and they very likely would be in a much higher tax bracket than the college-bound child.

SUMMARY

Positives: As a result of these legal, often-used deductions and transactions, here's a summary of what was accomplished for business owner Mike:

- He saves Social Security Tax contributions on the salary paid to the business owner's spouse and children.

- The children may be exempt from Social Security Tax because they are under 18, and Judy, as the owner's spouse, may be over the Social Security maximum because of her full-time job. The spouse's overpaid FICA tax will be refunded.

- Mike and Judy have lowered their overall income taxes.

- They pay some educational expenses with the tuition reimbursement plan and the stock given by his parents.

- All of the family's co-pays, eyeglasses and other out-of-pocket medical expenses, are now being paid with expense dollars from the business as an employee benefit.

- The child could be in a much lower tax bracket.

- The grandparents avoided capital gains taxes.

This scenario, which worked for Mike and his family, could lower overall college expenses for families with more than one child by many thousands of dollars, and allow them to avoid possible interest payments on college loans. In addition, all three generations enjoy combined savings.

Negatives: Most of the tax techniques mentioned here can apply only if one of the parents is self-employed or runs a business. Grandparents must have the cash or invested assets in order to take advantage of the tax savings through gifts to their grandchildren.

H. Roger Daisley

CHAPTER 12: Limited Payment Life Insurance Policy

An alternative idea I have been presenting to some of my clients has no 529 Plan limitations or penalties. The investment, a limited payment life insurance policy, would be the same as any other college funding investment methods mentioned already, but with these advantages:

- The parents control the asset as long as the parent thinks it is appropriate to do so, unlike most of the other plans discussed where the child has total control of the money accumulated for college at age 18 or 21.

- It builds cash value which you can borrow (up to 92%), or take by cashing in the policy. (Borrowing is usually better.)

- If you've purchased a form of whole life insurance from a mutual company which is owned by its policy owners, you continue to receive dividends that you can take in cash, leave with the insurance company to accumulate interest, or use to buy paid up insurance which adds to the death benefit and cash value of the policy.

- Should the owner of this asset—the parent or grandparent—die prior to accumulating the total amount intended, there is a death benefit (a payout) that would provide the amount the parent started out to save, NOT just the amount accumulated up to the time of death. (The other investment plans mentioned so far would only have the amount accumulated until the death of the primary income earner.)

- There is an optional disability benefit that will waive payments if the premium payer becomes totally disabled, thus guaranteeing the money will be there when the child is ready for college, assuming the parent and or grandparent is under the age of 65, the age when the waiver of premium ends for most companies. Even though premiums are waived, cash values still grow and you continue to receive dividends as if you paid the premiums yourself.
- It substantially minimizes market risk, because the cash value of the policy is guaranteed.
- It not only could pay for a child's education, but also could pay of the education of that child's child, because the cash values will continue to grow after your child has completed college.
- It could even supplement the child's retirement, because dividends earned after retirement could be paid to your child as declared each year.

How It Works—Parents

1. Purchase a limited payment life insurance policy on the primary income earner, with the waiver of premium benefit. The cash value will accumulate income tax-free.
2. If the primary income earner dies, the death benefit could provide money both to raise the child and still have money for college.
3. If the primary income earner becomes totally disabled, the waiver of premium benefit will allow the money to accumulate into the plan so the full

amount will be there for the child for college expenses.

4. Assuming the insured parent stays healthy and doesn't die, transfer the policy to the child—with the parent retaining ownership—under the "transfer of lives" provision. Typically, this would happen when the child started college. The reserves released will be sent to the parent, and the parent can use the reserves for college expenses.

Now the child has a life policy on their own life for which, under the premium offset provision, the child may never have to pay any premiums. Yet that insurance plan could continue to grow, possibly providing enough for the grandchild's education. (With a premium offset provision, the dividends declared will pay the premiums. Although this is not guaranteed, once a policy is in force for 15 to 20 years, there is usually a sufficient amount of accumulated dividends to pay the current and future premiums.

Additionally, the dividends would make a nice supplement to the child's retirement, assuming a participating policy (one that pays dividends) was purchased.

Cash values are guaranteed, which minimizes risk. And although dividends are not guaranteed, once they are declared, they become guaranteed as well.

This plan works best for very young children, from birth to about age five. If the children are older, there is another approach, again using a different limited payment life insurance plan.

For older children, I have suggested that parents buy the policy they can afford, but apply only about half the amount to be contributed in premium to the base policy, and the rest of the premium should be applied to something called a paid-up additions rider. The paid-up additions rider simply provides additional paid up insurance and increases the cash value much more quickly. Of course, they should keep the waiver of premium benefit on the rider premium as well as the base policy.

Life insurance policy dividends are not usually taxed as income, but if left on deposit, the interest earned is taxable. Therefore I usually recommend using the paid-up additions dividend option.

The uniqueness of this plan is that it builds cash values right away. When it is time for college, the parent can take the money out of the policy. This reduces the death benefit by the amount borrowed from the plan, but it keeps the policy in force, and then the loan can be re-paid so that the parent can use this money to supplement their retirement.

Some advisors use an indexed universal life policy which guarantees a minimum set interest rate, but can pay a higher interest rate if the insurance company has better investment returns.

How about a combination plan? Tax benefits *and* Life insurance. Purchase a life insurance policy on one parent's life, as listed above. When it's time for college, refinance your home (or take a second mortgage), then pay back the mortgage with the dividends from the life insurance policy, assuming they're large enough to do so. You get a tax deduction for the mortgage interest paid. Your policy continues to grow and will supplement your retirement while keeping a death benefits for final expenses.

How It Works—Grandparents

If the grandparents want to contribute, they can take a "10 Pay" life policy (pay premiums for only 10 years) on the life of the grandchild, with the parents being the beneficiaries. This accumulates cash value for college, but the premium is totally paid in ten years.

The policy cash values could be borrowed to pay college costs, and the dividends could repay that loan.

And then at the appropriate time, the policy ownership would be transferred to the grandchild. Imagine that grandchild receiving a dividend check each year. When he or she is eighty years old, the "child" will still be receiving a dividend. It would be like getting a birthday card from grandma and grandpa with money in the envelope, long after the grandparents are gone.

Caveats

- Although the industry has an excellent history of paying dividends, they aren't guaranteed until paid. While cash values of this type of policy are guaranteed, dividends are NOT guaranteed until after they have been declared.

- These specific advantages apply only to limited payment participating life insurance policies purchased from a mutual life insurance company. Mutual life insurance companies earn a profit, and that profit (divisible surplus) is distributed to the policy holders as dividends. The owners of mutual companies are the policy holders and they "participate" in the profits of the company.

- Stock companies, on the other hand, have stockholders who earn the profits of the insurance company. Purchasing a life insurance policy from a stock company does NOT make you a stock holder; you must buy stock in the company to be a stock holder. Policy holders do not participate in the profits, although there are some stock companies that issue "participating" policies. In addition, though you may get a loan on your policy, there are no dividends on "non-participating" policies, as there are with mutual company's "participating" companies.

Mike & Judy and Family

Mike did purchase a policy on his own life—for Jane's education. He purchased a "Paid-up at 65" policy. When Jane is 18 years old, under the "exchange of lives" provision, he will transfer the policy to Jane's life. The release of the reserves should be able to pay for her college education.

Jane will then have a "life-paid-at-65" policy that, due to the premium offset provision, she will not have to pay premiums out of her pocket, as the dividends could be large enough to pay the premiums for her. Don't forget the part about dividends not being guaranteed. Should the dividend be lower than expected, the balance between the premium and dividend will need to be paid.

Assuming that Jane gets married when she's 30 years old, and has a child by the time she is 35, the cash value and dividends on Jane's policy could be enough to help pay for her own child's college education.

Additionally, when Jane hits age 65, since all premiums will been paid, the dividends as declared each year by the insurance company could be payable to Jane to supplement her retirement income.

Mike also bought a policy on his life when Sarah was eight years old, about four years ago. It was a "Life paid-up at age 85" policy, and he wanted to put $1,000 a month into it. So, we put the minimum amount possible into the base whole life policy and the maximum amount into the paid-up additions rider.

Mike is accumulating money in that plan so that when Sarah goes to college in five years, he can borrow money from the policy to pay for at least some of her education expenses. And after Sarah is finished with college, he can use the dividends to pay back the policy loan. Mike plans to continue putting money into this policy to accumulate supplemental funds for his retirement.

Unfortunately, at the point I began working with Mike and his family, Michelle was already too old for them to take advantage of this type of planning. However, I am happy to report that they have found ways to pay for Michelle's college expenses using a combination of the tax planning discussed earlier, several small scholarships, financial aid, and contributions from her grandparents.

The Grandparents

George and Lydia, who were eager to contribute to their grandchildren's education, bought the "10-Pay" life insurance policy (10 years of premiums) on the lives of Sarah and Jane, with the parents, Mike and Judy, as the beneficiaries and owners. George and Lydia know that they're not going to live forever, but feel fairly certain they'll be around for at least 10 years and will be able to contribute the premiums for these plans during that time. They are looking forward to attending Sarah's college graduation ceremonies.

When it's time for Sarah, and then Jane, to go to college, money can be borrowed from these policies and the loan created can very possibly be re-paid by the dividends from these policies.

Once these loans are repaid, all future dividends can be sent directly to the grandchild. And if and when the policies are transferred, the grandchild could be receiving dividend checks even when they are in their 80s.

While there are certainly other options when it comes to using limited payment life insurance for helping to fund a child's—or grandchild's—education, these are the ones that worked for Mike and Judy's family.

CHAPTER 13: Summary

Here's another idea that I always suggest to families like Mike and Judy's. Wouldn't it be nice to be able to give your college graduate a free trip to Europe as a reward for having achieved a college education, and congratulations for the fact that they are about to embark on a career and independent life of their own? And wouldn't it be nice if maybe mom and dad and grandma and grandpa, could take that European vacation too? They've earned it!

So, here's one last idea I'll leave you with: Use a credit card with non-expiring frequent flyer miles to make tuition payments and pay for other college expenses. Very likely, there will be enough miles accumulated, after four years, to fund that vacation trip. Just make sure that the frequent flyer miles are of the *non-expiring* type.

Be Sure To Work With A Professional

There are many different methods for saving money to pay for your son's or daughter's education. In fact, there are so many different methods to consider that I highly advise you to seek the advice of an experienced specialist in this area.

Should you talk to your accountant? Perhaps, but only if your accountant has had specialized college funding training and is current in his or her knowledge of tax laws and regulations.

Should you talk to the college financial aid office? Remember, the business of college is to sell education, not give it away. If the person you are getting advice from is being paid by the school, you should question their incentive for helping you find ways for avoiding having to pay for tuition at their school.

Should you talk to your banker? Your stockbroker? What training have they had? Remember, their training in a particular product or service is important, but more importantly, your adviser needs to be knowledgeable about all the options available.

You need to be aware of all the options available and how they would work in concert with your overall financial plans and goals and how they work together. Your accountant may know about tax advantages, and the accountant's software may include American Opportunity or Lifetime Learning Credit options for calculating certain formulas. Your stock broker may know about 529 and Coverdell Plans. And your banker may be able to help you purchase U.S. Savings Bonds. Financial Planners from several disciplines might be very well-rounded in many aspects of financial planning, but are they specialists?

If you have a routine medical problem, you would start by seeing your GP or family internist. However, if you have serious heart trouble, you would want to see a specialist, a cardiologist. If you had cancer, you would want to see an oncologist. It is no different with college funding and retirement planning. And these are two of the biggest expenses you will incur in your lifetime.

And last of all, you need to start planning and saving now. Today, not tomorrow. Now!

Even if you think you may not be able to save as much as you actually should be saving, start saving now anyway, just start with a lower amount. The miracle of compound interest will work for you, and you will then have more options available. The longer you wait, the more you'll have to spend or borrow when it is time for your child—or grandchild—to attend college. If you wait until then, there will be many fewer options available to you.

Here is a proverb you've probably heard: The journey of 1,000 miles begins with one step. Take that step now. You can adjust the journey as tax laws and school regulations change. But get a plan, and start now!

Appendix A: The Investment Pyramid

The following are two examples of the many "Investment Pyramids" used by various financial consultants to help you see at a glance the risk levels of various types of investments. The least risky investments are at the bottom of the pyramid, and the most risky are at the top.

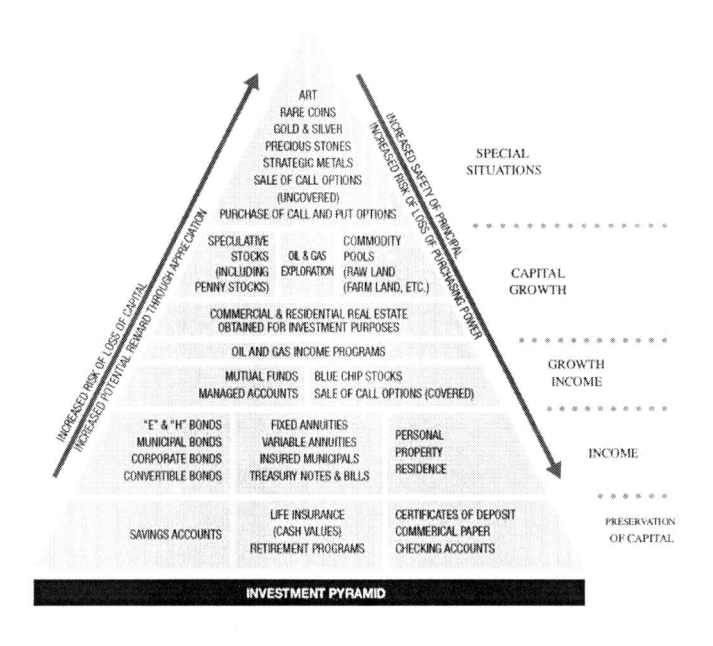

```
                           ART
                        RARE COINS
                       GOLD & SILVER
                      PRECIOUS STONES              SPECIAL
                      STRATEGIC METALS            SITUATIONS
                     SALE OF CALL OPTIONS
                        (UNCOVERED)
                  PURCHASE OF CALL AND PUT OPTIONS
              SPECULATIVE          COMMODITY
                STOCKS    OIL & GAS   POOLS
              (INCLUDING EXPLORATION (RAW LAND        CAPITAL
              PENNY STOCKS)         (FARM LAND, ETC.) GROWTH
              COMMERCIAL & RESIDENTIAL REAL ESTATE
              OBTAINED FOR INVESTMENT PURPOSES
                  OIL AND GAS INCOME PROGRAMS
                                                      GROWTH
               MUTUAL FUNDS    BLUE CHIP STOCKS       INCOME
              MANAGED ACCOUNTS  SALE OF CALL OPTIONS (COVERED)

            "E" & "H" BONDS     FIXED ANNUITIES
            MUNICIPAL BONDS    VARIABLE ANNUITIES   PERSONAL
            CORPORATE BONDS    INSURED MUNICIPALS   PROPERTY     INCOME
            CONVERTIBLE BONDS  TREASURY NOTES & BILLS RESIDENCE

                               LIFE INSURANCE    CERTIFICATES OF DEPOSIT
                                (CASH VALUES)    COMMERICAL PAPER      PRESERVATION
            SAVINGS ACCOUNTS  RETIREMENT PROGRAMS CHECKING ACCOUNTS     OF CAPITAL

                          INVESTMENT PYRAMID
```

(Increased risk of loss of capital / Increased potential reward through appreciation on the left side; Increased safety of principal / Increased risk of loss of purchasing power on the right side)

Source: Dearborn & Creggs Investments

Appendix A: The Investment Pyramid—*continued*

Higher Potential Risk
Higher Potential Reward

```
                    Art
                   Metals
                 Gem Stones
                   Options
                 Commodities
                 Exploration
                Venture Capital

                  Speculative

              Equity Partnerships
             Investment Real Estate
          Growth Stocks and Mutual Funds
          Variable Life Ins. and Annuities

                    Growth

             Sale of Covered Options
              Conservative Equities
     (Utility Stocks, Convertible Bonds, Balanced Funds)
         Residence   GNMA Retirement Plans
         Corporate Bonds    Municipal Bonds
             U.S. Govt. Notes and Bonds

                    Secure

   Savings  T-Bills  Fixed Equity Index Annuities  Fixed Annuities
              Money Market Funds/Accounts
         Traditional Life Insurance (Cash Values)

                   Foundation
```

Lower Potential Risk
Lower Potential Reward

Note: This pyramid is intended solely to illustrate a concept; it is not a promise of investment performance. Investors may differ on the risk level to which a particular asset is assigned. Before making any investment in mutual funds or variable annuities, you should be sure to read the appropriate prospectus or offering documents for a complete discussion of the fees and risks involved.

Source: ECA Marketing

Appendix B: Highlights of Education Tax Benefits for Tax Year 2010

The following charts highlight some differences among the benefits discussed in this publication. See the text for definitions and details. Do not rely on these charts alone.

	Scholarships, Fellowships, Grants, and Tuition Reductions	American Opportunity Credit	Lifetime Learning Credit	Student Loan Interest Deduction	Tuition and Fees Deduction	Coverdell ESA[1]
Benefit	Amounts received may not be taxable	40% of credit may be refundable (limited to $1,000)	Credits can reduce amount of tax you must pay	Can deduct interest paid	Can deduct expenses	Earnings not taxed
Annual Limit	None	$2,500 credit per student	$2,000 credit per tax return	$2,500 deduction	$4,000 deduction	$2,000 contribution per beneficiary
What expenses qualify besides tuition and required enrollment fees?	Course-related expenses such as fees, books, supplies, and equipment	Course-related books, supplies, and equipment	None	Books, supplies, equipment, room & board, transportation, other necessary expenses	None	Books, supplies, equipment, expenses for special needs services, payments to QTP. Higher education: room & board if at least half-time student, K–12 education, tutoring, uniforms, transportation, computer access, supplementary expenses
What education qualifies?	Undergraduate & graduate, K-12	1st 4 years of undergraduate (postsecondary)	Undergraduate & graduate, courses to acquire/improve job skills	Undergraduate & graduate	Undergraduate & graduate	Undergraduate & graduate; K-12
What are other conditions apply?	Must be in degree or vocational program; Payment of tuition and required fees must be allowed under the grant	Can be claimed only 4 tax years (including years Hope credit claimed); Must be enrolled at least half-time in degree program; No felony convictions	No other conditions	Must have been at least half-time in degree program	Cannot claim both deduction & education credit for same student in same year	Assets must be distributed at age 30 unless special needs beneficiary
In what income do benefits phase out?	No phase-out	$80,000 – $90,000; $160,000 – $180,000 for joint returns	$50,000 – $60,000; $100,000 – $120,000 for joint returns	$60,000 – $75,000; $120,000 – $150,000 for joint returns	$65,000 – $80,000; $130,000 – $160,000 for joint returns	$95,000 – $110,000; $190,000 – $220,000 for joint returns

Source: IRS Publication 970
[1] Any nontaxable distribution is limited to the amount that does not exceed qualified education expenses.

Appendix B: Highlights of Education Tax Benefits for Tax Year 2010 —*continued*

Caution: You generally cannot claim more than one benefit for the same education expense.

	Qualified Tuition Program (QTP)[†]	Education Exception to Additional Tax on Early IRA Distributions[†]	Education Savings Bond Program[†]	Employer-Provided Educational Assistance[†]	Business Deduction for Work-Related Education	Limited Payment Life Insurance Policy
Benefit	Earnings not taxed	No 10% additional tax on early distribution	Interest not taxed	Employer benefits not taxed	Can deduct expenses	Dividends not taxed
Annual Limit	None	Amount of qualified education expenses	Amount of qualified education expenses	$5,250 exclusion	Amount of qualifying work-related education expenses	No limits
What expenses qualify besides tuition and required enrollment fees?	Books, supplies, equipment, room & board if at least half-time student, expenses for special needs services, computer technology, equipment, and Internet access -2010	Books, supplies, equipment, room & board if at least half-time student, expenses for special needs services	Payments to Coverdell ESA; Payments to QTP	Books, supplies, equipment	Transportation / Travel, other necessary expenses	No limits
What education qualifies?	Undergraduate & graduate	Undergraduate & graduate	Undergraduate & graduate	Undergraduate & graduate	Required by employer or law to keep present job, salary, status, maintain or improve job skills	No limits
What are some of the other conditions that apply?	No other conditions	No other conditions	Applies only to qualified series EE bonds issued after 1989 or series I bonds	No other conditions	Cannot be to meet minimum educational requirements of present trade/business; cannot qualify you for new trade/business	No limits
In what income range do benefits phase out?	No phase-out	No phase-out	$70,100 – $85,100; $105,100 – $135,000 for joint and qualifying widow(er) returns	No phase-out	No phase-out	No limits

Source: IRS Publication 970, with information about Limited Payment Life Insurance Policy added by the author.
[†] *Any nontaxable distribution is limited to the amount that does not exceed qualified education expenses.*

Suggested Reading

Books & Articles

"Bank on Yourself" by Pamela Yellen; www.bankonyourself.com

"Becoming Your Own Banker" by R. Nelson Nash; www.infinatebanker.org

"Ethical Considerations in College Admission Practices: A Proposal for Dialogic Involvement," by Victoria Gallagher. *The Journal of College Admission*, Fall 1992.

"How to Pay Wholesale for College" by Andrew Lockwood; www.andylockwood.com

"How Privatized Banking Really Works," L. Carlos Lara and Robert P. Murphy, available on www.usatrustonline.com

"Killing Sacred Cows" by Garrett Gunderson, www.killingsacredcows.com

"Strategies to Help Grandchildren Now, Not Later," by Deborah L. Jacobs, The New York Times, October 29, 2009

"Tips to Avoid Bait & Switch in the World of Financial Aid," by Doug A. Schantz, posted on www.cheapscholar.org March 11, 2010

"Wealth in the United States," Wikipedia, www.wikipedia.com

Tax Publications

www.irs.gov and www.taxalmanac.org

IRS Publication 950—"Introduction to Estate and Gift Taxes"

IRS Publication 970—"Tax Benefits for Education"

Internal Revenue Code: Sec. 72: "Annuities, certain proceeds of endowment and life insurance contracts"

Web Sites

www.treasurydirect.gov — U.S. Dept. of the Treasury website

www.federalstudent-loanstoday.com —offers tips for getting federal student loans; aggregates links to other sources of scholarships and financial aid.

www.finaid.org — The Smart Student Guide to Financial Aid; provides information about various funding options, such as UGMA / UGMT.

www.fra.com — Financial Resource of America; financial services firm specializing in the financial and retirement needs for retired Americans.

www.prb.org — Population Reference Bureau; information about world and by-country population, health, and the environment.

www.savingforcollege.com — Your Guide to Saving For College.

www.ssa.gov —The Official Website of the U.S. Social Security Administration.

www.staffordloan.com — A Service of the Student Loan Network.

H. Roger Daisley

About H. Roger Daisley

H. Roger Daisley is an experienced leader in the financial services industry, having served at every level, from sales to agency manager to senior vice president, at the most respected mutual companies, including New York Life, MassMutual, The Guardian, and Security Mutual.

An experienced speaker, Daisley has lectured at many colleges and universities, and for groups such as CPAs, attorneys, and business owners, on topics ranging from investing, tax law changes, educational funding, long term care, estate planning, and the marketing of financial products.

This is Roger's first book, but he has extensive experience writing journal and magazine articles, and has contributed chapters to several textbooks published by one of the oldest organizations for financial industry training, The American College. He has also been interviewed on NBC for a three-part series on retirement planning.

He has been an executive officer of three prominent financial services organizations, and officer and/or board member of several of the industry's key professional organizations: NAIFA, GAMA, FPA, and the American Society of CLU's and ChFC's.

Roger attended the U.S. Naval Academy at Annapolis, and has two Masters of Science Degrees and eight professional designations. He is currently an officer and board member of the South Bay Cruising Club, a Long Island yacht club, and an officer and board member of the Alzheimer's Association of Long Island.